ESSENTIAL LIFE SKILLS FOR BOYS

Essential Life Skills for Boys

EVERYTHING YOU NEED TO KNOW TO THRIVE AT HOME, AT SCHOOL, AND OUT IN THE WORLD

SCOTT TODNEM

ILLUSTRATED BY
MARTHA SUE COURSEY

ZEITGEIST • NEW YORK

This book is possible because of Alayna, Kyle, Elliott, and Chase. Thanks for the inside jokes, constant insight, and lifelong learning. Extra thanks to Zeitgeist for the continued opportunity to share words with the world.

Published in the United States by Zeitgeist Young Adult, an imprint of Zeitgeist™, a division of Penguin Random House LLC, New York.
zeitgeistpublishing.com

Zeitgeist™ is a trademark of Penguin Random House LLC
ISBN: 9780593690451
Ebook ISBN: 9780593690024

Illustrations by Martha Sue Coursey
Book design by Emma Hall
Author photograph © by Ashley Summers

Printed in the United States of America
1st Printing

CONTENTS

PUT YOUR BEST FOOT FORWARD

HEY, PAL! Glad you picked up this book. You must be interested in developing life skills, and this book is a big step in the right direction.

By learning life skills, you begin a path to independence and earn the trust of your parents or caregivers. This has huge benefits—it will probably result in more freedom, greater self-reliance, more confidence, and improved relationships with family and friends.

I know all this because I'm a health education teacher. I work with hundreds of students each year as they manage the shift from childhood to adulthood. I help boys your age learn to handle situations with accurate information and a good sense of humor. (You'll notice I'm a little sarcastic at times. I might even call you dude, dude.)

Throughout this book, you'll learn how to prepare for adulthood. Each chapter covers a bunch of skills under a general topic—for example, you'll learn how to wash your athletic shoes in the cleaning chapter and cut an onion in the cooking chapter. Feel free to bounce around depending on your interests and needs.

Everyone has unique living circumstances, which means that some of these directions will need tweaking. You may not be able to use or purchase everything listed. Also, different households have different rules. That's okay—change things up to work for you. Talk to a trusted adult if you have questions, and be careful with anything even potentially dangerous.

Here's your challenge: Learn as many life skills as possible and mark them off on the checklist on the next page (and the checklist at the beginning of each chapter).

Let's get started!

LIFE SKILLS CHECKLIST

- Pack your lunch
- Make your bed
- Set the table
- Change a lightbulb
- Take care of your pet
- Sew a button
- Tighten a screw
- Change batteries
- Sort clothes
- Wash clothes
- Remove laundry stains
- Dry clothes
- Iron clothes
- Fold laundry
- Clean shoes/wash sneakers
- Wash and put away dishes
- Sweep, Swiffer, Mop
- Vacuum
- Dust
- Take out the trash
- Clean the bathroom sink and mirror
- Clean the shower/tub
- Clean the toilet
- Use a plunger
- Use kitchen tools
- Use kitchen appliances

- Put out a kitchen fire
- Cut an onion
- Boil pasta
- Sleep tight
- Move your body
- Eat right
- Adopt healthy habits
- Practice first aid
- Visit the doctor
- Visit the dentist/orthodontist
- Cope with stress
- Understand your emotions
- Think and respond
- Keep body odor away
- Shower
- Care for your hair
- Shave
- Care for your skin
- Protect your teeth
- Keep a schedule
- Set up for school success
- Master homework
- Ask for help
- Resolve conflicts with authority figures
- Have a good conversation
- Show empathy

- Apologize
- Resolve conflicts
- Set and keep healthy boundaries
- Deal with group conflicts
- Use social media wisely
- Enjoy time alone
- Spend wisely
- Save wisely
- Budget
- Understand and manage a bank account
- Leave a tip
- Donate
- Communicate online
- Make and receive phone calls
- Text with care
- Email with care
- Write a thank-you note
- Use good manners
- Read a map
- Pack a suitcase
- Host a hangout
- Be a great guest
- Watch a younger child
- Pick and wrap a present
- Tie a necktie

PART ONE
AT HOME

Life skills begin at home, so let's start by talking about things like cooking, cleaning, eating, and sleeping. Not sure how to make your bed? Need to remove a stain from your favorite T-shirt? Confused by a can opener? Want to learn basic first aid? The answers are in the following pages.

CHAPTER 1
AROUND THE HOUSE

- PACK YOUR LUNCH

- MAKE YOUR BED

- SET THE TABLE

- CHANGE A LIGHTBULB

- TAKE CARE OF YOUR PET

- SEW A BUTTON

- TIGHTEN A SCREW

- CHANGE BATTERIES

PACK YOUR LUNCH

Getting your lunch ready for school? First, decide when's the best time. Should you make it the night before? Or build it fresh each morning? Either way, here's how to make and pack it.

1. Make a sandwich or pack leftovers for the bulk of your lunch. Consider the three big calorie providers— carbohydrates, proteins, and fats. These "macronutrients" help you function at your best. Read food labels to learn more. And did you know different colored foods pack different vitamins?

2. Find snacks to round out your meal. You may have prepackaged foods at home—stuff like granola bars, crackers, cheese sticks, yogurts—plus fresh fruits or veggies, like apples, bananas, grapes, or carrots. Avoid loading up with junk food and sugary foods; they can drain your energy. But don't be afraid of calories. Mix things up and vary your meals each day.

3. Toss your lunch, a water or other drink, and an ice pack (if needed) in a paper or reusable bag. Nice work!

MAKE YOUR BED

Making your bed sends a message to your brain every morning that you're ready for a great day. It kickstarts your daily routine, proves you have discipline, and only takes a couple of minutes to accomplish. Pretty nice benefits for such a small task.

1. If you're making a bed from scratch, starting with clean sheets, begin with the fitted sheet (the part with the elastic). Lift each corner of the mattress to place the elastic corners underneath. This sheet may be tight, so it might take some strength and practice. If it keeps slipping, put it on opposite diagonal corners first to help.

2. Next, put on the top flat sheet. Stand by the long side of the bed, hold one side of the sheet, and flap it up and over the bed. Allow it to settle all lined up the way you want it. Line the top of the sheet up with the head of the mattress and let the sides of the sheet hang over the sides of the bed.

3. Put your blanket(s) on top of the sheet. You can either 1) line up the top edge of the blanket with the top end of the sheet, or 2) lay the blanket a little lower and fold the top side of the sheet down over the blanket. Next, tuck in the bottom of the sheet and blankets (and the sides, if you want). It's kind of like finishing wrapping a birthday present with gift wrap.

4. If you have a top comforter or bedspread, lay it over the blanket, tuck in the bottom/sides if you want, and fold it down about 4 inches at the head of the bed for a nice, finished look.

5. Put the pillow in its pillowcase, pop it on the bed, and you're ready for the day. (By the way, it looks great!)

SET THE TABLE

If you're setting the dinner table for just your family, it will look different from a formal dinner table for guests. Here's how to set the table for you and your family.

1. Put placemats around the table, one for each family member, or lay a tablecloth over the table, adjusting it to make sure it hangs pretty evenly on each side.

2. Place a dinner plate in front of each chair.

3. Lay a napkin to the left of the plate (folded is nice!).

4. Place a fork on the napkin.

5. On the right of the plate, place the knife next to the plate, blade facing inward toward the plate, and then the spoon right outside the knife.

6. Directly above the knife, place a drinking glass.

7. Bonus points: Ask your caregivers if they want you to set out any condiments (ketchup, butter, salt and pepper, and so on).

CHANGE A LIGHTBULB

Lightbulbs have come a long way—especially those LED and smart lightbulbs that you can link to your home Wi-Fi.

1. Safety first! Before changing a lightbulb, turn off the light switch. Use a step stool or ladder if needed. Also, check with your caregivers before working on anything electric.

2. Check the watts label on the burned-out bulb. There are common wattage bulbs like 60 or 100 watts, but some light sources might use fluorescent bulbs or other styles.

3. Install the new bulb. Some bulbs screw in; others are pushed or twisted into place.

4. Dispose of the old bulb in a trash can, or put it into another bag first to avoid it breaking in an open garbage bin.

5. Fluorescent and CFL bulbs contain mercury. If these break, a trusted adult should open windows for ventilation, wear a mask, and wipe up (not vacuum) the broken pieces into a sealed bag. Different towns have different rules for disposal—if possible, bring the bulb to a recycling center.

TAKE CARE OF YOUR PET

Are you a pet owner? If so, cool! We'll cover cats and dogs here. (For other animals, refer to an animal store expert for caregiving help.) Caring for your pet can be broken down into three areas:

- **Food.** Cat owners can generally leave cat food out so your cat can eat when they're hungry. Dog owners usually need to limit the amount of food put out, since dogs tend to overeat. Ask your vet to suggest the right type, amount, and time(s) of day for your size and breed of pet. Most important, cats and dogs should always have clean water available. Treats and some "people food" may be fine, but definitely watch the portion size and types of foods—you don't want to cause an upset stomach, especially if you're the one cleaning up their potty breaks, if you catch my drift. Some foods are toxic to dogs, including chocolate, grapes, raisins, onions, and garlic, to name a few. Ask your veterinarian any questions you have about foods.

- **Exercise.** Learn your pet's exercise and play habits—for instance, does your pet need outside time? To be walked? How often? How about toys to play with? Think about how you can connect with your pet. Your pet and your family will benefit from your involvement, and so will you! It's true—this social connection can boost your overall mood and well-being.

- **Grooming.** Does your dog or cat need brushing? Ask your caregiver if you can help with simple grooming tasks. Dogs also need regular nail clippings and baths. These are things a caregiver can teach you, but be aware that a dog's nails can bleed (a lot!) if cut too short.

Whether you have a cat, a canary, or a cow, taking your pet-caring responsibilities seriously and showering them with love is a win-win situation!

SEW A BUTTON

Did you lose a button? No worries—here's an easy step-by-step guide to getting buttoned back up.

1. Find a thread color that matches your garment. Thread a needle with about a foot of thread, then make a knot at the end of it.

2. Start from the back of the fabric. Push the threaded needle through to the front and through one of the buttonholes and pull it all the way through. Cross the needle over and through another hole, going back through the fabric to your starting spot. Repeat this several times to ensure the button is secure. On a four-hole button, go in any pattern you like—try a crossed "X" thread pattern for best results. You can also wrap the thread around itself between the bottom of the button and the fabric. It creates space for the button to be, well, buttoned!

3. Once done, double- or triple-knot the thread on the inside of the fabric and cut off the remaining thread. All set? You bet.

TIGHTEN A SCREW

Let's talk about two main types of screwdrivers and screws: flathead and Phillips head. The tip of a flathead screwdriver looks—you guessed it—flat. Flathead screws have one slot at the top. These can slip a bit during use, which is why Phillips heads were invented. Phillips head screwdrivers have a tip shaped like a plus sign. Let's go over how to use them.

- To tighten a screw, insert the tip of the screwdriver into the slot on the top of the screw and turn clockwise.

- To loosen a screw, insert the tip of the screwdriver into the slot on the top of the screw and turn counterclockwise. Helpful tip: Remember "righty-tighty, lefty-loosey"—in other words, turn a screwdriver handle to the right (clockwise) to tighten a screw. Turn it to the left (counterclockwise) to loosen a screw. There are occasional exceptions to this rule, but it's a helpful phrase to remember.

CHANGE BATTERIES

From toys to flashlights to wireless remotes, battery-powered devices are everywhere. Many of these items are now rechargeable, thanks to lithium-ion batteries. But if you need AA, AAA, C, or D batteries, here's a quick how-to.

- Double-A (AA), triple-A (AAA), C, and D batteries each have a positive- and negative-charged end. The end that pops up in a circle, like on the head of a Lego minifigure, is the positive pole. The flat end is the negative pole. Match the poles to the plus and minus signs inside the device and push the batteries into place.

- If there's a spring inside the device, that usually touches the negative pole. Stick that end in first—it's easier this way.

- Batteries usually alternate so they are upside down next to each other.

- Small rectangular batteries are 9-volt batteries. They have "terminals" on the top that snap into matching terminals on the device. Push hard to snap those into place.

WHAT'S THAT BEEP?

Smoke detectors and carbon monoxide detectors usually come with detailed instructions. If the device begins beeping loudly and constantly, this indicates a smoke, fire, or carbon monoxide emergency. If the device is making short chirps, it usually means the battery is low. Some alarms have built-in batteries, so the whole system may need replacing; others take 9-volt or AA batteries. If you replace the batteries, test the alarm to make sure you've done it correctly. Hold the button down until you hear the alarm. As always, double-check with your trusted adults if you have questions about keeping your home safe from fire and poisonous gas, and have an emergency plan in place.

CHAPTER 2
RINSE AND REPEAT

- SORT CLOTHES
- WASH CLOTHES
- REMOVE LAUNDRY STAINS
- DRY CLOTHES
- IRON CLOTHES
- FOLD LAUNDRY
- CLEAN SHOES/ WASH SNEAKERS
- WASH AND PUT AWAY DISHES

- SWEEP, SWIFFER, MOP
- VACUUM
- DUST
- TAKE OUT THE TRASH
- CLEAN THE BATHROOM SINK AND MIRROR
- CLEAN THE SHOWER/TUB
- CLEAN THE TOILET
- USE A PLUNGER

SORT CLOTHES

Doing your own laundry is kind of a big deal. It might not be that much fun, but you'll gain independence by having clean clothes when you want them. (You know that favorite shirt you love to wear over and over again?) Whether you have access to a washer and dryer at home or go to a laundromat, the same steps generally apply.

1. **Separate your clothing.** It's up to you, but typically you'll want to have three piles: whites/lights, darks, and heavies (hoodies, jeans, and towels). This will ensure that brighter or darker colors don't "bleed" onto your light-colored clothes and your heavy jeans won't wrinkle your T-shirts in the dryer.

2. **Check your pockets.** Don't forget that pack of gum—or worse, your phone! Zip up zippers so they don't snag your other clothes.

3. **Treat stains.** Spray or rub stain remover or detergent on any stains before you put the clothes in the washer. (See Remove Laundry Stains on page 26 for more information.)

WASH CLOTHES

Whether washing clothes in the machine or by hand, you'll want to treat your clothes right. Here's how.

WASHING MACHINE

1. **Set water temperature and wash cycle.** Most times, you'll use a simple warm water/cold rinse cycle. But hot/warm water kills more bacteria than cold water, making it best for cleaning after an illness. Cold water is safe for all colors, while hot water may fade bright or dark colors. Select whatever wash settings your caregivers use or follow the directions on your clothing tags.

2. **Add detergent.** With a top-loading washer, use either the dispenser compartment or add the detergent directly to the drum (the basin that holds the clothes). Front-loading washers usually have a detergent drawer. Be careful not to use too much detergent, and never place pods in a detergent drawer. Pods go right in with the water and clothes. If you use liquid fabric softener, add that to the dispenser or drum before the start of the cycle or before the final rinse of the wash cycle.

3. **Wash clothes.** Put your clothes in the drum and press Start.

HAND-WASHING

Camping in the woods? On vacation? Or just don't have access to a washer and dryer? No problem! You can always hand-wash and hang dry your clothes.

1. Fill a tub or sink with warm water and add a small amount of detergent (about 1 teaspoon). Use a little more detergent to treat any stains.

2. One item at a time, submerge and soak the clothing, then gently move the garment around.

3. Drain the tub and refill it with clean, cool water. Rinse and repeat until the soap is removed.

4. Wring out as much water as possible, then hang, drape, or lay your garment flat over a towel (but not on wood or fabric furniture).

REMOVE LAUNDRY STAINS

The top tips for removing stains:

* Pretreat stains before you wash your clothing.

* Treat stains as quickly as possible so they don't become permanent.

* Make sure the stain is gone before putting your clothes in the dryer. The dryer can make stains permanent, too.

Here are some common stains and how to deal with them.

* **Grass or mud:** Got a stain remover? If so, spray it on your clothing and let it sit for around 15 minutes before popping your clothes into the washing machine. You can also mix one part vinegar with two parts water (such as 1 tablespoon vinegar with 2 tablespoons water) and rub the mixture into your clothes with a scrub brush or old toothbrush before washing.

* **Ink, marker, or paint:** If paint, ink, or permanent marker has dried into your clothing, you might be out of luck. But you can always try! Move fast to get the clothes wet and repeatedly scrub the fabric under running warm water. Then wash as usual.

* **Blood:** Wet your clothing with cold water and rub or scrub with a brush until gone. If that doesn't work, blot hydrogen peroxide directly onto the stain and rinse it away.

DRY CLOTHES

Drying clothes correctly is a simple—but important—life skill.

1. **Clean the lint trap** (the screen that collects fuzz from your clothes). Do this by removing the lint and returning the trap to the slot.

2. **Move them along.** Once the washer cycle ends, untangle your clothes and pop them in the dryer as soon as you can. Take out any clothes that shouldn't be dried and either hang them or lay them flat (read the tags for drying instructions). If you let them sit for too long in the washing machine they can develop mildew, and that's kind of stinky. If that happens and you notice a moldy smell, rewash the clothes.

3. **Choose the drying cycle and push Start.** That's it.

4. **Remove and fold.** When you remove your dry clothes from the dryer, carry them or put them in a laundry basket to bring wherever you will fold them, and clean out the lint trap for the next user.

IRON CLOTHES

Want to look good and put together when dressed up? Smooth out those wrinkles in your clothes!

1. Ask your caregiver if you need to iron your clothes, and get their permission. You can use the iron dry (without steam) or with steam. (To use steam, you'll fill a small compartment in the iron with water and press a little button to create steam. That steam helps press out creases and wrinkles. Just be careful; steam can burn you.)

2. To start, set up your ironing board and place the iron on top so the pointy tip of the iron is facing up. Plug it in and set the temperature knob to the setting for the fabric you're ironing. Check the tags on your clothing to make sure they can be ironed.

3. Spread your garment flat in a single layer on the ironing board. Slide the shirt or pants over the narrow end of the ironing board so only a single layer is lying flat on the board. Holding the iron by the handle, slowly move the iron over the fabric until the wrinkles disappear. Move the fabric as needed to iron all the sections. Never leave the iron sitting in the same spot for more than a few seconds. It can start a fire.

4. If ironing a button-down shirt, use the narrow part of the ironing board to iron inside the shoulders and sleeves as well as the collar area. Iron everything flat before folding the collar into its normal position.

5. End by pressing the iron against any creases that are supposed to be there, like on the front of dress pants.

6. Once you're done ironing, unplug the iron, set it upright on the ironing board, and let it cool far away from anything flammable.

FOLD LAUNDRY

Folding your clothes soon after you take them out of the dryer (rather than crumpling them up and shoving them in the drawer—*no, you'd never do that!*) helps your clothes look nice. Here's how.

- **Pants:** If hanging them, fold them in half so the legs meet and then drape them evenly over the hanger. If not, fold them so the legs meet, then fold them in half so the waistband meets the bottoms. Fold them once more so one pocket is facing you. Pop them in a drawer.

- **T-shirts:** Two options here: 1) Fold the shirt in half (vertically), line up the sleeves, fold the sleeves together and behind the shirt, then fold the whole shirt down in half. 2) Lay the shirt facedown on your bed, and fold vertically in thirds. Fold down in half; any graphics on the shirt will be facing up.

- **Collared shirts:** You probably want to hang these. If you can't, button one of the top buttons and then fold it similarly to a T-shirt. Smooth out any wrinkles as you go.

CLEAN SHOES/ WASH SNEAKERS

Whatever you just stepped in—poop or a puddle—there's a way to get your shoes clean.

- **Dirty shoes:** Wet a cloth with water and rub your shoes to remove any surface dirt you can, or go outside and knock your shoes on the ground or against each other.

- **Wash and dry:** Yes, you can put some sneakers in the washer and dryer. That's best for cloth or mesh shoe material (like running shoes and casual footwear).

- **Leather shoes:** If your shoes are mostly leather, wet a cloth with water and a gentle soap (like Ivory) and carefully scrub the shoe. Wipe away extra soap with another damp cloth and dry the shoe with a clean, dry cloth.

- **Stepped in dog poop:** Sorry to hear that! Use a hose and a disposable rag or a handful of paper towels outside to spray and scrub the bottoms. Do it as soon as possible so you don't smell it all day—or worse, track it indoors.

WASH AND PUT AWAY DISHES

You'll score points at home if you help with dishes after meals.

DISHWASHER

1. Scrape off any leftover food and rinse before loading dishes into the dishwasher.

2. Load dishes without blocking each other. Use the lower rack for big items like plates and the upper rack for items like glasses and smaller bowls. You can save space by lining up plates in the same direction.

3. Place silverware in the utensil basket. Don't let the utensils nest together or block each other. Place forks and knives in the basket with the handles up to avoid poking the person emptying the dishwasher.

4. Fill the detergent container with the correct amount of dishwashing detergent, then shut the container and the dishwasher door. Lock the dishwasher door.

5. Select the right cycle button (your caregiver can guide you) to start the machine.

6. Bonus points: Empty the dishwasher when it's done!

HAND-WASHING

1. Scrape any leftover food off the dishes.

2. Soak pots and pans in hot water and dish soap for a while to loosen any stuck-on food.

3. Fill a clean sink or basin with very warm water. Add dish soap.

4. Wash plates, glasses, utensils, and pots and pans, starting from the least dirty to the dirtiest.

5. Use a soapy scrub brush, sponge, or cloth to clean your dishes. You might need some elbow grease (remember, that's muscle!) here. Don't use a rough sponge or scouring pad to clean nonstick pots and pans—this can scratch them.

6. Make sure to clean both sides of plates, the undersides of bowls, and all surfaces of glasses and cups—especially where you put your mouth.

7. Carefully clean utensils, focusing on the part you put in your mouth.

8. Rinse all dishes in clean, warm running water before putting them in a drying rack or drying them with a clean towel.

SWEEP, SWIFFER, MOP

Hardwood, linoleum, and tile floors need to be swept nearly every day, especially if you have pets. You might not be able to see the dirt, but it's there!

1. Start by moving clutter off the floor you plan to sweep.

2. If you don't have a vacuum cleaner (or if your family doesn't use one on these kinds of floors), sweep all those little pieces of dirt, leaves, food, and random trash into a pile with a broom. It may take a few swipes to pick up little remnants of dust.

3. Sweep the pile into a dustpan and dump the debris in the trash.

   Less often, you'll need to wash high-traffic areas. Focus on corners in the kitchen, by your entryway, under the table, and so on.

- **Mop and bucket:** Fill a bucket halfway with water and the amount of floor cleaning liquid directed on the label. (Too much soap might make the floor slippery.) Dip your mop in the bucket, wring out the water, clean a section of floor, and rinse the mop to clean the next section. Replace the water when it gets dirty so you're not just pushing dirty water around. Fill the bucket with clean water and wipe or mop the floor clean when you're done washing.

- **Swiffer:** If you're using a Swiffer or similar type of mop, attach the wet cloth to the mop as directed on the package of cloths and clean the floor in small sections, working your way back toward the doorway. Replace the cloth when it gets dirty.

- **Scrub brush and bucket:** If you wash on your hands and knees, have a bucket of soapy water nearby and use plenty of elbow grease with a scrub brush. Replace the water when it gets dirty, and wipe the floor with a damp cloth when done.

VACUUM

Are you in charge of vacuuming? Or do you want to be?

1. Before you start, pick up any clutter or clothing from the floor to clear the area.

2. Choose the floor setting (low/hardwood, medium/low-ply rugs, high/thick carpet), plug in the vacuum, and turn it on.

3. Make slow, multiple back-and-forth sweeps to give the vacuum a chance to suck up dust and dirt. With carpet, you might be able to see the vacuum lines, which makes it easier to see what you've covered. Be careful not to let the vacuum suck up thin rugs, low-hanging curtains, or cords; they can damage the machine.

4. If needed, use the hose and the other attachments to clean tight spots like under furniture, on stairs, and in corners.

5. When you're done, turn off the vacuum, unplug it, wrap up or retract the cord, and put it away.

6. If you're feeling adventurous, carefully empty the vacuum bag or canister—just don't spill all the dirt you vacuumed up!

DUST

Dusting is a good way to earn points for trust, and it's a cleaning habit that goes well with vacuuming. In fact, dusting first allows the vacuum to pick up any dust that falls on the floor.

1. Choose your tool for dusting: a damp cloth or paper towels (for non-wood surfaces), microfiber cloth, or any handheld duster. Handheld dusters are nice because they have handles to help you reach high corners and behind shelves.

2. Starting high and working your way down, use your tool to clean off everything—tables, bookshelves, cabinets, clock faces, wall decorations and artwork, window blinds, windowsills, entertainment centers, lamps, and even the tops of kitchen appliances.

3. Pick up framed photos and trinkets on shelves, dust them and the shelf underneath them, and then put them back in place.

4. Toss or clean your dusting cloth.

TAKE OUT THE TRASH

Are you in charge of emptying the trash in your home? There's an art to this!

1. Start by emptying trash bins from the kitchen, bedrooms, and bathrooms into a garbage bag—but not overfilling the garbage bag, because then it's harder to close.

2. Tie the garbage bag closed with a knot or use a twist tie so it doesn't spill.

3. Carry (don't drag it—the bag can break) the trash outside to the garbage can (or wherever it goes).

4. For recycling, sort the paper and plastic (and anything else your community recycles) according to the community's rules. On collection day, take items wherever they are picked up.

5. If you have specific garbage days each week, consider doing the work the night before. Like, make it part of your routine after homework and before bed. Text friends, play a video game, take out the trash. Boom. MVP.

CLEAN THE BATHROOM SINK AND MIRROR

Here's one you'll love: cleaning the bathroom! Joking aside, it needs to be done, my friend. A clean bathroom looks and smells good; plus, it's good for your health, decreasing germs that spread illness. Choose an antibacterial cleaner for best results. And never mix bleach and ammonia products—that's a toxic combination.

SINK

1. Remove everything on the counter.

2. Spray the counter and faucet with a cleaning spray and wipe them with a sponge or cloth. You can also use a cleaning wipe.

3. Next, spray and wipe the basin (the part that holds water). Get all those little toothpaste bits wiped up.

4. Put everything back on the counter.

MIRROR

Spray a cloth with glass cleaner and then wipe the mirror. (It's better for the mirror than spraying directly on the mirror.). Weirdly, using a newspaper instead of a cloth reduces streaks.

Use a new rag or cloth after you clean each part of the bathroom. (You don't want to wash *anything* with a cloth you used to clean the toilet!)

CLEAN THE SHOWER/TUB

Just as you need to get clean, your shower and tub need to get clean, too.

1. If you have a shower with glass doors, spray glass cleaner on the inside of the doors and wipe them down with a clean cloth to get rid of streaks and soap scum. If you have a shower curtain, pull it to one side.

2. Spray the walls, inside the tub, the faucet handle(s), the downspout, and the rim of the tub with cleaner (pick up any soap, shampoo, etc. so you can clean underneath them) and wipe everything down with a clean cloth or sponge. You may need to use a little elbow grease to get the tub clean, especially in the corners. Rinse everything with clean water.

3. Every couple of weeks, spray and wipe down the shower head in addition to your other cleaning.

4. Wipe everything dry to prevent mildew stains.

CLEAN THE TOILET

It's gotta be done, man. Use disposable disinfecting wipes or a cleaning spray with a cloth or sponge (that you use only for these tasks). Use new wipes and clean cloths (or clean the sponge) for each part of the toilet. Have a garbage bag handy for any disposable items you may have used to clean the toilet bowl.

1. Pour toilet bowl cleaner into the toilet bowl as directed. Let it work its magic as you clean other parts of the toilet (in the following order!).

2. Spray and wipe the top of the tank and the flush handle.

3. Spray and wipe the outside and inside of the lid.

4. Spray and wipe the top, then bottom, of the toilet seat, then the toilet bowl rim.

5. Spray and wipe the outside of the toilet bowl and the surrounding floor.

6. Using your toilet bowl brush, clean the inside lip and inside of the toilet bowl. Replace the brush in its holder.

7. Flush—you're done!

USE A PLUNGER

There's no pretty way to put this: Sometimes the toilet gets clogged. For reasons we won't detail here, you may find yourself in an emergency situation where you need a plunger. Better to know what to do ahead of time, right? If you catch things before an overflow, you can avoid a dirty disaster.

1. Find a plunger. Different plungers have different bottoms, but the idea is the same: to create suction around the hole where everything gets flushed down.

2. Place the rubber bottom of the plunger over the hole to cover the hole completely.

3. Use the plunger handle to push the plunger down and up quickly, with force, multiple times, without lifting the plunger. Do this until it sounds like the water's draining down the hole.

4. Flush the toilet to make sure the clog is gone. If not, repeat the steps above.

5. If the clog won't go away and the water looks like it will overflow, get grown-up help.

WEAR, SLEEP, REPEAT?

Generally, you can wash your jeans after every four or five wears, or if they start to smell. Although it may sound gross, a smell test works fine! Check to see that odor isn't lingering after a few days of wear. More active days = more sweat, so that will require an earlier wash. If you're regularly active in your jeans, wash them more often, but if you're mostly just working through a school day or hanging out with friends indoors, you can probably go through multiple wears over a two-week span before washing.

CHAPTER 3
COOKING UP KNOWLEDGE

- ■ USE KITCHEN TOOLS

- ■ USE KITCHEN APPLIANCES

- ■ PUT OUT A KITCHEN FIRE

- ■ CUT AN ONION

- ■ BOIL PASTA

USE KITCHEN TOOLS

Kitchen skills will allow you to make meals and entertain friends and family. Let's start with some basic kitchen tools.

CAN OPENER

1. Electric: Lift the top handle, then slide the can into place, positioning the lid under the blade. Bring down the top handle so the magnetic seal touches the lid, and press down to start. (Proceed to step 5.)

2. Manual (non-motorized): Place the can opener's small circular blade firmly inside the top edge of the metal can.

3. Squeeze the can opener's handles together. You should hear a pop.

4. Turn the crank clockwise, away from you. The can opener will move around the top of the can, cutting it open as it moves.

5. Once fully cut, carefully remove the lid. Watch for sharp edges!

CONTINUED

CUTTING BOARD

Cutting boards protect countertops and keep foods clean when cutting. Many families keep separate cutting boards for different foods (like one for meat and one for fruits and veggies). Plastic boards are dishwasher-safe; hand-wash wood boards in warm, soapy water.

KNIVES

Let's explore the two main kinds of blade: Serrated knives have pointed "teeth" for cutting fruits, vegetables, and breads. Non-serrated knives have a straight-edge blade, great for cutting meat.

To cut with either, set your food on a cutting board. Holding the knife handle firmly with one hand, begin pressing into the food with a back-and-forth sawing motion. If it's meat, use a fork to hold the meat still. For fruits, veggies, or bread, hold the food with your other hand, keeping the knife away from that hand. Never cut toward yourself.

POTS AND PANS

- Pots: deep cooking vessels, used to boil foods in liquids (like potatoes, soup, or pasta)

- Pans: shallow, used for things like scrambling eggs, making pancakes, or sautéing vegetables or meats

- Large shallow pans: for casseroles, brownies, and cakes

- Large flat or rimmed pans (baking/cookie sheets): for baking rolls, pizzas, and yep, cookies

- Muffin pans: contain cups that can be filled with muffin or cupcake batter

USE KITCHEN APPLIANCES

You need to know how to use your kitchen appliances—and how to use them safely.

MICROWAVE

1. Make sure your dish is microwave-safe—never use metal.

2. Cover your food with a paper towel, plastic wrap, or upside-down plate if it might splatter (not foil!).

3. Arrange food evenly on the dish. Cut larger foods into smaller pieces to heat through.

4. Choose your power setting and cook time.

   - Are you heating or defrosting? Choose the right button (ask for help if needed).

   - Push the buttons for the suggested heating time and then push Start. Cook times depend on the microwave's wattage. When in doubt, start short (30 seconds), remove your food and stir it, then microwave for additional time as needed.

5. Carefully remove your food from the microwave. Watch out for scalding steam when uncovering.

6. If food spilled or splattered in the microwave, wipe it clean with a wet paper towel.

TOASTER

1. Plug it in and choose your desired setting (how dark you want your toast).

CONTINUED

2. Pop your bread in the designated slots.

3. Press the lever down and wait for your bread to pop up. Never touch the inside heating wires with your fingers or utensils.

4. Unplug the toaster, let it cool, then dump out any crumbs.

TOASTER OVEN

1. Choose the settings according to what you're cooking (oven temperature, time, toast vs. cook).

2. Place food on the grates or, if messy, use a foil-lined tray.

3. Press Start. Stay nearby while the food cooks.

4. When done, use potholders to remove the food or tray.

BLENDER

1. Add the ingredients, starting with liquids and soft items, then any frozen ingredients.

2. Pop on the lid and press your desired setting to start.

3. If needed, stop the blender, open the lid, and press down any solid foods with a spoon. Add more liquid if needed. Cover and restart.

4. Once done, pour your drink into a large glass.

5. Rinse all parts (careful with the blade!) and either hand-wash the container or put it in the dishwasher.

PUT OUT A KITCHEN FIRE

Fires are scary. But they're less scary if you know what to do. If a grease fire starts in the oven or on the stove, don't use water to try to put it out. That will only spread the fire. First, turn off the heat, call an adult to help, and try the following methods.

- **Baking soda:** Tossing baking soda on a small fire in the oven or on the stove will help smother the flame. Know where the baking soda is stored so you can grab it if needed.

- **Fire extinguisher:** Pull the pin and squeeze the handle, aiming the nozzle at the base of the fire. If you have a fire extinguisher, look it over so you know how it works.

- **Metal lid:** Cover a small stovetop fire with a metal lid if possible. Fire cannot exist without oxygen. Be sure to use a metal lid—glass will shatter.

- If you can't smother the flames and the fire is getting bigger or spreading, call 911 and get everyone outside quickly.

CUT AN ONION

You've probably heard that cutting an onion will make you "cry." To avoid tears, place a damp towel or full bowl of water next to your cutting surface. The water will soak up some of the chemical gases the onion releases. Now, let's get cutting!

1. Get your tools ready: cutting board, bowl, and sharp straight-edged knife big enough for the onion.

2. Cut the onion in half. Cut off the ends and remove the skins—throw those away.

3. Keeping the cut sides down on the cutting board, cut lengthwise through the onion from root to stem.

4. Hold the onion firmly with your fingers curled out of the way of the knife. Make cross cuts and dice into the size you want. As you make cuts, try to keep the onion together to avoid releasing the tear-causing fumes. Watch your fingertips and knuckles!

5. Place the chopped onions in a bowl, away from your eyes. Don't touch your face!

6. Wash your hands.

BOIL PASTA

Different pastas have different cook times. Is it spaghetti? Penne? Linguini? Ravioli? Fresh, frozen, or dried? See the packaging for directions.

1. Fill a large pot halfway full with water. Add salt for flavor (optional).

2. Cover the pot and turn the burner heat on high until the water is boiling.

3. Uncover, add the pasta, and cook uncovered for the time stated on the package. Stir often, scraping up any pieces that stick to the bottom of the pot.

4. When the cook time is over, remove a piece of pasta with tongs, run it under cold water, and eat it to test if it's done.

5. Once the pasta is done, turn off the heat and remove the pot from the stove with potholders (get permission first). Carefully pour the contents away from you into a colander in the sink.

6. Shake the colander to drain the water.

7. Pour the pasta back into the pot, add butter, sauce, or olive oil, and enjoy!

COOKING IT RIGHT

It's important to preheat an oven so your food cooks at the right temperature—otherwise it might be undercooked (yuck). Different ovens have different buttons, so ask your caregiver to show you how yours works. Usually it means setting the temperature you want (sometimes there's also a Start button), and waiting (for about 15 minutes). An alarm may go off when it's ready. Once your oven reaches the desired temperature, it's ready for your food. Just be sure not to leave the oven door open for too long, or the heat will escape.

CHAPTER 4
SOUND BODY, SOUND MIND

- SLEEP TIGHT

- MOVE YOUR BODY

- EAT RIGHT

- ADOPT HEALTHY HABITS

- PRACTICE FIRST AID

- VISIT THE DOCTOR

- VISIT THE DENTIST/ORTHODONTIST

- COPE WITH STRESS

- UNDERSTAND YOUR EMOTIONS

- THINK AND RESPOND

SLEEP TIGHT

Did you know that your brain and body both benefit from a good night's sleep? The human brain matches new information with previous experiences during sleep and dreams. It's an incredible process of merging memories that can only happen with the right amount of rest—plus, you won't be a walking zombie the next day. At your age, 8 to 10 hours a night is ideal.

- **Create a routine.** Try sticking to regular sleep and wake times. This means weekends, too. You can't sleep for 5 hours one night and 12 the next and expect to feel good. There's no such thing as "catching up on sleep." Either you get the sleep you need for the day, or you don't.

- **Set the mood.** A dark, cool, and quiet room is best for sleep. Use a fan or gentle music to drown out distractions (not music from headphones).

- **Ditch your devices.** Screens are sleep enemies. Stop using screens an hour before bedtime—it'll program your body for sleep.

MOVE YOUR BODY

Everyone knows that physical activity is good for you. But do you realize *everything* it does? Exercise benefits your heart and bloodstream, strengthens your muscles and bones, and helps you sleep. It also helps you do well in school, cope with stress, and manage emotions. Exercise provides physical challenges and gives you time to hang out with friends. And it's fun!

- Aim for an hour or more of physical activity every day. This can be all at once or added up as the day goes on.

- Make sure some of your movement is intense enough that you notice your heart beating. Break a sweat!

- Try to make exercise fun so you'll stick with it. Play a sport or game you love, go for a walk or run with friends, exercise to your favorite tunes—anything you like.

- If you break a sweat, finish off that workout with a shower so you smell as good as you feel.

EAT RIGHT

Spoiler alert: Food rots.

Just a little humor to remind you that real, whole foods don't last forever. They eventually go bad. Food that rots is actually a good thing, because it means that at its best, it's fresh and full of nutrients. You want to eat food *before* it goes bad! Let's check out some eating-well basics.

- **Get enough of the three calorie providers.** These are carbohydrates (like whole grains, potatoes, and corn), proteins (like meats, nuts, and eggs), and fats (like healthy oils, avocados, and nuts). Combined with water, and vitamins and minerals from foods, these nutrients ensure you can function at your best.

- **Enjoy food.** Food can be fun; plus, it provides the energy you need to do all the things you want to do.

- **Aim for a "colorful" plate.** This will ensure you're getting a wide range of nutrients. Which of these foods do you love to eat?

  - Red foods help the heart, eyes, and skin and fight disease and illness (strawberries, cherries, raspberries, red peppers, watermelon, tomatoes).

  - Orange foods help the eyes and circulation and fight disease and illness (oranges, carrots, sweet potatoes, orange peppers, peaches, cantaloupe).

  - Yellow foods help cell growth, gut health, and the heart and eyes (lemons, papayas, corn, pineapples, yellow peppers, mangoes).

- Green foods fight illness and help the bones and reproductive system (spinach, avocados, broccoli, zucchini, lettuce, green beans).

- Blue/purple foods help with tissue repair and circulation, and fight disease and inflammation (blueberries, cabbage, plums, blackberries, eggplant, prunes).

ADOPT HEALTHY HABITS

Two of the very best habits you can form for good health are really simple.

WASH YOUR HANDS

Sorry, licking your fingers clean after eating potato chips doesn't count! We're talking soap and water here, pal. Keeping your hands clean is the number-one way to prevent contagious disease. Wash your hands before eating and after using the toilet. Wash them regularly when you're sick or around someone who is sick. And wash them after you've played with pets or touched any animals.

1. With soap and warm water, scrub your palms, fingers, and backs of your hands. Get in between your fingers, too.

2. Scrub for at least 30 seconds. Pick your favorite tune to hum. Do this every day to keep the germs away!

DRINK PLENTY OF WATER

Next to oxygen, water is the substance you need the most. "Hydration" means having enough water in your body and constantly replacing any lost water. Proper hydration helps with digestion and circulation. It regulates body temperature and gets rid of toxins. It helps your muscles and joints and allows you to think clearly. Water may not have a taste, odor, or color, but it sure has an impact!

A good daily water goal? Around eight 8-ounce cups of water. Try these tips to reach that 64-ounce goal:

- Start each day with a big glass of water.

- When you pass a drinking fountain in school, take a sip.

- Bring a big thermos of water to sports activities. Drink enough to feel good.

- Feeling tired? Try half a glass of water. Bored? Try another half a glass of water. Annoyed or frustrated? Drink some more water, bud. Sometimes a little hydration is all you need.

- Not all your water has to come from water! Watermelons, oranges, and other juicy fruits and beverages including seltzer, tea, and fruit juices (in moderation—they're high in sugar) all provide water to the body.

PRACTICE FIRST AID

Knowing how to administer first aid is a valuable life skill! (Get an adult immediately if the injury is serious.) Make sure you know where to find first aid supplies in your home and how to use them. These include:

- Adhesive bandages, gauze, and similar wraps in different sizes

- Adhesive tape

- Antibiotic ointments and antiseptic wipes

- Thermometer

- Tweezers

- Nonlatex gloves

- Over-the-counter medications (like acetaminophen and ibuprofen)

- Heat and cold packs

- Scissors

You can make a first aid kit with these supplies and put it where you can find it fast. Also, make a list of emergency contacts like your doctor and poison control, with phone numbers, and post it for all family members to quickly find in an emergency. Here are some basics:

- **Cuts:** For a minor cut, wash the area gently with soap and water, dry, then cover with a bandage. For a cut that doesn't stop bleeding right away, apply pressure to the area with a clean towel. You can hold that body part up higher to slow the bleeding. Tell a grown-up.

- **Splinters:** Use tweezers to gently pull out the splinter, pulling at the same angle as the splinter. After removing, wash the area with soapy water.

- **Nosebleed:** Sit down (don't recline or lie down). With one hand, gently pinch the nose shut, right above the nostrils. Hold a tissue against the nostrils if needed. Don't peek. Wait 10 minutes to see if the bleeding has stopped.

- **Burns:** Get the burned area under cool water quickly. Call for help. Never apply creams, oils, or butter to burns.

- **Beestings:** These can be serious for people who are allergic. Call a grown-up or 911 for help. If you are alone and there seems to be no problem (besides it just hurting like heck), quickly scrape the stinger out with your fingernail (if it's there) and place a cold pack or ice over the sting.

VISIT THE DOCTOR

Time to see the doctor? Whether you're going for your annual checkup or an illness or injury, consider these pointers to make sure you get everything you need.

1. It's your body, so make a list (written or mental) of everything you've noticed that doesn't feel right: congestion, indigestion, pain, and so on. Be honest about your symptoms (even if they're embarrassing).

2. Know that the doctor will respect your privacy. If you want your discussion to stay confidential, tell your doctor. Ask as many questions as you like—they are there to help you. You may want to write down your doctor's instructions to help you remember them.

3. It's normal to feel uncomfortable talking about personal stuff with the doctor. But remember, doctors have heard it all before. Take a deep breath and ask away. Your body matters, and you have the right to know.

VISIT THE DENTIST/ ORTHODONTIST

Today's dentists and hygienists are trained in gentle and effective ways of cleaning and repairing teeth and gums.

1. They will inspect your teeth and gums. Share any concerns.

2. They may apply a mild anesthetic to numb the area they're working on. Then they'll use a variety of tools to remove plaque buildup and clean your teeth and gums.

3. They'll usually polish the teeth and apply fluoride to strengthen them. Oh, and they might gift you a new toothbrush and floss. Cool.

4. Your dentist may recommend an orthodontist. Orthodontists correct overbites, underbites, and crooked or out-of-place teeth.

Some additional oral-care wisdom:

- Visit the dentist twice a year to help keep your mouth healthy.

- Wear retainers as directed so your teeth don't shift back to their original position.

- Don't wrap your retainer in a napkin. There's probably a giant retainer graveyard out there with all the retainers that accidentally got thrown in the school cafeteria's garbage.

- Hopefully you've got these teeth for life. Taking care of them now means the best chances of this happening.

- Braces or no braces, let your smile shine bright!

COPE WITH STRESS

School, family, friends—all these things can lead to feelings of stress and anxiety. First, know that you're not alone—everybody feels stressed out sometimes. Also, not all stress is bad. Some challenges can lead to success. But when stress becomes too much and you need help dealing with it, try these strategies:

- **Talk with a trusted adult.** Find someone you trust—a parent, favorite aunt or uncle, teacher, counselor—and tell them how you're feeling. If the first person you talk to isn't helpful, find someone else.

- **Breathe deep.** During times when you're really stressed, taking slow, deep breaths tricks your body into thinking it's calm. Breathe in for a count of four, hold it for a count of four, breathe out for a count of eight, hold for a count of four. Repeat until calm.

- **Practice mindfulness.** Simple activities like going outside for a walk without distractions, or focusing all your senses on the food you're eating or the dog you're petting, can help you become calm. Focus on what you're doing at that moment.

- **Meditate.** Search YouTube for "free guided meditations." These teach you how to calm down and chill out in the moment by using your mind.

- **Exercise.** Moving your body creates feel-good hormones and can improve your mood and reduce stress. Get out there and run, jump, toss a ball, swim—whatever you like!

- **Unplug.** Social media and video games can increase stress. Limiting screen time helps you be more in tune with your surroundings and less stressed, rather than sucked into drama (real or virtual!).

- **Get sleep.** We talked about this earlier, but it's worth repeating that sleep helps the body and mind function better. This isn't just grown-up talk—it's proven research!

UNDERSTAND YOUR EMOTIONS

We all have lots of emotions—every day, every hour. How often do you think about your emotions? When you feel over-whelmed, it can be really helpful to get to know your emotions so you can deal with them. Let's learn how.

1. **Identify your emotions.** To start, simply identify your feelings. How do you feel? Are you having a new emotion? Good, bad, or in between? That's the first step.

2. **Name your emotions.** Next, identify the emotion by giving it a name. Labeling it helps you control how to respond. Find describing words—more than just "fine" or "normal." What, specifically, is the emotion? Excited? Embarrassed? Hurt? There is power in giving your emotions a name (you'll learn why below).

3. **Understand your emotions.** After identifying and naming your feelings, the next step is to understand them. This can be done quickly in the moment, or it might take days and weeks. Think about the possible cause of them. For example, why are you feeling sad? Was it a bad grade on a test? A missed shot that lost the game? A mean comment from a classmate? A pet passing away? Once you figure this out, you can work out a way to cope with the tough emotion.

4. **Express your emotions.** You've figured it out: the emotion, the name of it, the reason for it. Now express it! Say you're upset because you missed a shot that lost the basketball game. Tell someone you trust. Maybe it's a caregiver or a good friend. You can even express it to yourself. Say, *"Dude, I missed that shot. I'm so mad."* Hopefully you'll get a good response (even from yourself), like *"Hey, you made four other points, and six assists, and two steals—you didn't get that final shot, but you still did well. Practice more for next time!"*

THINK AND RESPOND

Now that you know how to identify, name, and understand your emotions, you can choose how and when to respond. You may have already reacted to the emotion (like cringing inside when you missed that shot), but responding is different. Your reaction is involuntary, which means you couldn't choose or control it. A response, on the other hand (such as storming off the court or laughing it off), occurs after a little more thought and time.

Here's how to respond in a helpful way:

1. **Pause for a moment.** If your instinct is to lash out or storm off, take a few deep breaths and rethink whether this is the right response.

2. **Choose your words.** Your body language helps, too. If you're feeling great, it's okay to show the world a smile. If not, you don't have to fake it. But you don't want to bring others down with you or do something you'll regret later. You can even say, *"I'm feeling very frustrated right now. I'm going to take some time alone until I feel more like myself. Cool?"*

3. **Check in with yourself.** Once you've expressed yourself, you can focus on regulating your emotions. That means keeping track of your feelings. It helps to watch out for them so you can change your behavior as needed or stop a poor response before it happens.

Once you're able to do this, pat yourself on the back. Feelings come and go, and instead of trying to ignore them, you're accepting and responding to them in a helpful way. And look, sadness and anger happen, just like pride and happiness. If you're not okay, it's okay to say so. Even to yourself. It might help to have a listening ear, however. Sometimes, all we need to do is vent or get a little support. Especially when things get too big to handle on your own, don't deal with it alone—find someone to talk to!

LOVE THOSE EARS, BUD

Earbuds and headphones—who doesn't love 'em? Problem is, they don't always love us. Listening to sounds that are too loud for too long can damage the eardrum by causing it to lose its sensitivity. You want to keep your hearing so you can enjoy all of life's great noises, from the calming sounds of nature to your favorite beats. So try not to have earbuds in too much, and avoid them altogether during sleep. Follow the 60-60 rule: Listen at 60 percent of max volume for no longer than 60 minutes at a time.

CHAPTER 5
KEEPING IT CLEAN

- KEEP BODY ODOR AWAY

- SHOWER

- CARE FOR YOUR HAIR

- SHAVE

- CARE FOR YOUR SKIN

- PROTECT YOUR TEETH

KEEP BODY ODOR AWAY

Have you noticed that when you're hot, your sweat glands spring into action? That's because sweat is produced on the surface of your skin to cool off. It evaporates into the air, pulling heat away from the body to cool you down.

The sweatiest parts of the body are your hands and feet. Other places get sweaty, too—one of those places is your armpits. Sweat doesn't actually smell bad; it's the mixture of sweat and bacteria that causes a stench. Let's talk about how to make sure your scent is a good one!

- If you aren't using deodorant already, it's time. Apply under your arms each morning, and after physical activity and showers.

- Try wearing clean clothes every day (especially clean underwear!) so your body stays clean and smelling fresh. Some items can be worn multiple times before washing, like jeans and sweatshirts. But clothes don't need to have visible dirt on them to be dirty. Most clothes need cleaning between uses.

SHOWER

Yes, dude, you need to bathe or shower every day to stay clean. Let's cover some important (but sometimes forgotten) points.

1. Wash your whole body. Don't just stand under the water. Scrub with a washcloth or loofah.

2. Soap will work for your skin and body hair, or you can shampoo your head and then use some of those suds to wash any body hair.

3. Ask your caregiver how often to wash the hair on that noggin of yours. A few times a week is a good start, but it may also depend on your style of hair and ethnicity.

4. If you have foreskin covering the head of your penis, gently pull that skin down to clean the area underneath. If you're circumcised, still clean around this area every day. Be careful, though; too much soap can also cause a burning sensation in the urethra, that tiny hole where urine comes out.

5. Afterward, rinse thoroughly with water. You're clean!

CARE FOR YOUR HAIR

Hair is closely connected with our heritage; you could even call it hair-itage. Your hair care needs depend on your hair texture.

- **Shampoo:** Shampooing regularly keeps hair clean and reduces oil buildup. Just get a good lather going and rinse thoroughly. Boys with Black hair textures may want to avoid harsh shampoos and seek out shampoos meant to be gentle, as many shampoos will dry the hair.

- **Conditioner:** If you use conditioner, only condition the ends (or the roots will get oilier). Don't condition oily hair. Same rules apply here as for shampoo: Lather well and rinse well.

- **Towel vs. hair dryer:** Use a hair dryer if you want to dry your hair completely or style it. Toweling your hair dry is easy—just towel, then comb. However, if you go to bed with a wet head, you're likely to wake up to a wild hairstyle. (Silk wraps are common for protecting the hair overnight in Black communities.)

- **Comb vs. brush vs. pick:** This depends on your preference and hair texture.

- **Hair care products:** Wax/pomade is good for sticking your hair up; gel is better for toning down curly styles. Hair oil can help with Black hair types. Ask your barber for suggestions for your specific hairstyle.

- **Haircuts:** Find pictures of hairstyles you like and show your barber. Just choose pictures featuring hair texture like yours.

SHAVE

How you maintain body hair is a personal choice. If you feel that it's time to start shaving your face, check with a caregiver who shaves, if possible, for guidance. Here's a short guide:

1. Choose a simple razor and shaving cream or gel.

2. Wet the area you're going to shave with warm water, then rub with a thin layer of cream or gel.

3. Press the razor against your skin with a little pressure. (Too light pulls the hairs. Too hard might cut the skin.)

4. Shave "with the grain" first. The "grain" refers to the direction that the hairs naturally point. Generally, this is downward on the face toward the neck. Never run the blade side to side—this will cut you.

5. Clear the razor with water after every few strokes.

6. Go back to any areas you missed. Shave against the grain now if you want.

7. Rinse with water and go out to "face" the world (pun intended!).

CARE FOR YOUR SKIN

Your skin is your protective layer, and it needs care, too. Let's talk about how.

- Wash your face twice a day, and trim your nails whenever needed. Use gentle soap to wash your forehead, cheeks, and around your ears.

- Protect your skin by using sunblock, especially in summer. Lighter skinned? Apply sunblock year-round when outdoors. Be sure to use an SPF of 15 or higher and apply a nickel-sized blob to your face and about 2 tablespoons to your entire exposed body. If you're using a spray, be sure to use enough so you see a sheen on your skin. Darker skinned? Sunscreen is equally important and should be applied the same way.

- Got acne? Acne happens when pores—small holes in your skin that grow hair and release sweat—become clogged with oil and dead skin and become inflamed as bumps that we know as pimples or zits. Doctors recommend leaving pimples alone—popping them can cause infection and scarring. If you can't stand to go out with a pimple, at least clean your hands first, and only squeeze if it has a small "head" on it. A pimple can be gently pressed to release the pressure under the skin. Wash the area, and use an acne cream as needed.

- Ask a caregiver to find a dermatologist (a skin doctor) if the acne seems severe.

PROTECT YOUR TEETH

You're a good-looking dude, so keep your mouth clean and
your smile bright!

1. Place your toothbrush, toothpaste, dental floss, and
    mouthwash in plain sight in your bathroom (so you
    remember your routine).

2. Brush at least twice every day to prevent gum disease and
    cavities. Aim to brush your teeth for two minutes each time.

3. Put a pea-sized amount of toothpaste on your toothbrush,
    then wet it.

4. Whether you're using a manual or electric toothbrush,
    brush in a circular motion on the front, top, bottom, and
    back of each tooth. Also brush the gums gently to help
    with blood flow and tooth health.

5. Brush your tongue, too—this fights bacteria and keeps your
    breath fresh.

6. Brushing won't remove all the plaque, so you'll need to floss
    between your teeth at least once a day. Floss between all
    teeth and up to the gum line.

7. Rinse out your mouth with water (or mouthwash), and
    you're done!

LOOK GOOD, FEEL GOOD

Guys your age start to develop their "look," which includes—but goes beyond—keeping clean and healthy. What's your style? Don't be afraid to try out different looks. Maybe you like graphic tees. Or clothing with sports teams. Maybe you enjoy dressing up in a shirt and tie—or just tie-dye! Experiment with clothing and find what makes you feel good. If you decide you want those expensive sneakers or designer clothes, maybe it's time to start practicing another life skill—working to earn money. Look into doing chores around your home, babysitting, mowing lawns, or dog-walking/pet-sitting for a neighbor (see page 116 for more ideas)!

PART TWO
AT SCHOOL

School becomes a big part of life at your age. It involves balancing family with friends. And balancing homework with activities. Oh yeah, and balancing emotions and challenges. It's a busy time, but you're up to the task. As time goes on, academics and relationships will become more demanding, but remember—as you get older, you get more capable!

Chapter 6 explores skills you can use to succeed academically, while chapter 7 talks about skills you can learn to succeed socially at school and in life. Let's go!

CHAPTER 6
ORGANIZATION 101

- KEEP A SCHEDULE

- SET UP FOR SCHOOL SUCCESS

- MASTER HOMEWORK

- ASK FOR HELP

- RESOLVE CONFLICTS WITH AUTHORITY FIGURES

KEEP A SCHEDULE

Between classes, extracurricular activities, and friends, life can be busy. This means you'll need to constantly manage your schedule. Here are some helpful tips:

- **Know where you're going.** Keep your class schedule with you. You'll probably memorize your schedule quickly, but a snow day or holiday can mess up the order of your classes, so it helps to have your schedule on hand.

- **Create a set study time.** Decide when you'll do homework. Are you better off doing it right after school? Or do you need a break? Maybe you're busy with extracurriculars and need to wait until after dinner. A routine will help keep you on track.

- **Keep a calendar.** If you're busy with after-school activities, keep a calendar—either on paper or on your computer or phone.

- **Plan ahead.** Put your completed homework in your backpack the night before it's due. Make your lunch the night before, too. Set your uniform, musical instrument, and other items you need by the door.

SET UP FOR SCHOOL SUCCESS

Now that you have different teachers for your various school subjects, you'll need to be better organized than ever before. No worries! A little preparation can go a long way.

- **Start strong.** Get organized in the first weeks of the new school year (and even before school starts) to help limit nerves and stress. What supplies do your teachers recommend (notebooks, folders, pens and pencils, and so on)? Gather them well before class starts and remember to bring in replacements as needed throughout the school year.

- **Limit distractions.** In class, try to avoid distractions like toys, habits like tapping pencils, even chatty classmates who take your focus away from the teacher and the lesson. Put your phone away until the bell rings. Make sure other people nearby, even friends, don't steal your attention. Try to keep the same focus when doing homework and avoid distractions.

- **Stay attentive.** Sit up straight and follow the teacher with your eyes. Listen closely to the teacher's instructions so you can follow through on expectations. Raise your hand and participate as much as possible—this will keep you interested (and the teacher will remember at report card time!).

- **Write down reminders.** Take notes from the lesson as well as any definitions or dates to remember. Write all of your homework assignments in one place and check your list of assignments each night.

- **Reset whenever needed.** When you feel like you're getting disorganized or falling off track, read over this section again. All these school skills—which also apply to life—will help if you need a reset at any point during the year.

MASTER HOMEWORK

Good homework habits are a key to school success. Here are a few homework helpers:

- **Keep track of your homework in one place.** Write down the homework for each class and when it's due.

- **Dedicate a place to do homework.** If possible, work at a desk or table (rather than on the floor or in bed).

- **Try to do your homework at the same time every day.** Stick to that time and it will become an effortless part of your daily routine.

- **Unplug.** Leave your phone and other distractions in another room while you concentrate on your homework.

- **Don't put it off.** Get it done! This way you'll have extra time at night to reward yourself. Do something relaxing: play sports or video games, jam on your keyboard, or whatever you enjoy best. (Turn off screens an hour before bed to ensure a good night's sleep!)

ASK FOR HELP

You might not know where your classes are on the first day of school. Your family might move, and you have to start at a new school later in the year. You might find a subject really diffi-cult. These are times to ask for help! Teachers, counselors, and other school staff members can lend a helping hand. Manners go a long way, my friend. If you're lost or confused, just say so politely.

Try these phrases as needed:

- *"Hi, excuse me. I can't open my locker. Can you help?"*

- *"I'm lost. Can you point me to the right classroom?"*

- *"I'm a little confused on this assignment. May I have more help on this part, please?"*

- *"I'm uncomfortable in this small group because we've had some major arguments. Is it possible to find a new place for me?"*

Notice how much better these questions sound than yell-ing, *"My locker doesn't work!"* or *"I don't know where to go!"* And they're more likely to get someone to help you.

RESOLVE CONFLICTS WITH AUTHORITY FIGURES

Your teachers, counselors, coaches, support staff, and administrators want to help you and see you succeed. And respect is a two-way street. This means that respect is gained by giving it. That said, conflicts do happen. What should you do if you have a disagreement with a teacher or other adult or get in trouble after making a mistake?

1. Listen carefully to first clarify the issue(s). Listen to learn, not to respond or defend yourself.

2. Be honest. If it's a disagreement, respond calmly and politely. If you made a mistake, admit it. Your maturity and honesty can go a long way in gaining respect.

3. Apologize as needed, making sure your apology is genuine and without blame.

4. Ask questions. Try *"How can I do better?"* or *"How can I avoid conflicts like this in the future?"*

5. Thank the adult for their time. Gratitude goes a long way—both in and outside of school.

TALK TO YA LATER

Let's face it—school is a social event. That can be a great thing, but don't let the social aspect stand in the way of your success. When other students distract you, it takes away from your ability to focus on the lesson. It also gets in the way of the teacher doing their job. Try to ignore distractions. If other students or nearby noises get in the way, ask to have your seat moved. Same goes for homework— tell your friends you'll talk to them later and hit Do Not Disturb on your phone. By letting your friends know that you prioritize schoolwork, you send a message about what's important to you—and might inspire them to do the same!

CHAPTER 7
FRIENDS, THROUGH BETTER AND WORSE

- ☐ HAVE A GOOD CONVERSATION

- ☐ SHOW EMPATHY

- ☐ APOLOGIZE

- ☐ RESOLVE CONFLICTS

- ☐ SET AND KEEP HEALTHY
  BOUNDARIES

- ☐ DEAL WITH GROUP CONFLICTS

- ☐ USE SOCIAL MEDIA WISELY

- ☐ ENJOY TIME ALONE

HAVE A GOOD CONVERSATION

We all have something to say. But the best conversationalists will tell you that having a conversation isn't just about talking. Being an active listener is key. Let's explore how.

1. Listen to understand (instead of listening to reply). Try to see the other person's point of view rather than waiting to jump on something they say.

2. Use positive body language: Face the speaker, make eye contact, and nod your head naturally to show understanding.

3. Ask questions as needed. Without interrupting, show an interest in another person's life in order to share in that experience.

4. Offer personal connections without trying to impress. Don't unnecessarily steal the focus.

5. Have a difficult topic to bring up? Try to choose a good time and place. Give some context beforehand, like *"Hey, I need to bring up something kind of tough. Do you have a minute?"* or *"I'm hoping we can talk about _____. That didn't make me feel good. Can we revisit that real quick?"*

SHOW EMPATHY

Empathy is the ability to understand another person's feelings, even if you haven't been through something similar. If you notice someone having a strong emotion surrounding a certain experience, use compassion. You've heard of putting yourself in someone else's shoes. Think, how would you feel if you were in their situation?

- **Respond helpfully.** Look for simple ways to lend a hand. With family, this could be offering to carry in groceries, clean your room, help with laundry, or just listen. With friends, this could be getting their mind off something by hanging out or doing an activity together, or providing a sympathetic ear.

- **Show care.** Ask, *"How can I help?"* You might not know exactly what's wrong. If something seems a bit off, ask if everything's okay and what you can do to make the situation better.

- **Do little things.** Kindness spreads, my friend. Open doors for people, pick up dropped items, invite other classmates into a group or activity if you notice they are alone.

APOLOGIZE

Did you make a mistake? Or did they? Either way, here's how to set things right:

- **Be specific.** Explain, *"Hey, I'm sorry about when I said _____. I didn't really mean it."* Or *"I apologize for the other day. That wasn't cool of me. Will you forgive me? Can we move past that?"*

- **Apologize without blame.** Don't add any "buts" (like *"I'm sorry I hurt your feelings, but you were annoying me."*). Also, stay away from a non-apology like *"I'm sorry you feel that way."*

- **Be up-front.** Are you the one who deserves an apology? You may not get what you want, but you can certainly ask. Say, *"I was really hurt when _____. I think I deserve an apology."* Notice how up-front and to the point that is?

- **Accept an apology with grace.** Even if you're hurt, recognize that the person apologizing is trying to make things right. Say, *"Thank you. I accept (or appreciate) your apology"* and move on.

RESOLVE CONFLICTS

Resolving conflicts isn't about winning or losing; it's about finding a respectful agreement that meets everyone's needs. If you find yourself in the middle of a conflict—a disagreement between you and a friend or former friend—try this course of action.

- **Take the high road.** Don't stoop to name-calling or other insults, even if the other person has.

- **Know when to step away.** If the conversation turns nasty, remove yourself from the situation as fast as possible. Try something like, *"Sorry if I hurt your feelings, but we aren't getting along, so I'm just gonna take off for now."* Keep your distance, and give the situation a little time to cool off. It usually helps.

- **Address the conflict.** When the time is right (and this may be right away), address the conflict calmly, such as *"Hey, I think things got out of hand back there. I felt like . . ."* Notice the use of the word "I." I-statements explain how you feel, rather than blaming with a you-statement.

- **Listen up.** There are two sides to every story, so try to actively listen to the other person without interrupting. You can respond in a way that shows understanding, like *"I'm sorry I upset you"* or *"I'm sure you didn't mean it that way."* If peace has been made, a handshake and a "no hard feelings" message communicates resolution.

- **Trust your instincts.** You probably have a good sense of what's right and what's wrong. If something feels off—unusual, concerning, or just plain weird—you might be right. If an interaction, in person or online, makes you uneasy, trust your gut. Don't try to resolve the situation on your own. Seek out a trusted adult immediately and tell them what's happening.

SET AND KEEP HEALTHY BOUNDARIES

Boundaries are an essential life skill! Setting boundaries involves something called consent. Consent means actively agreeing to an activity. You get to decide what happens physically, socially, and emotionally. And the same is true for others.

Consent means you don't feel pressured to do something you don't want to, and it means you don't pressure others into anything either. Consent creates comfort and respect for everyone. And that's a life skill to be used in all future interactions.

To set effective boundaries, it's important to be clear with your message. A few different approaches can help:

- **Use I-statements.** We talked a bit about this on page 94. An I-statement expresses your thoughts, feelings, and values as a sentence beginning with the word "I." This is a powerful tool for communication because it's direct. Say, *"I am not interested in going to that party"* rather than *"It's not a good time for me."*

- **Avoid you-statements.** Take blame away from others during conversation and especially during conflict by avoiding statements that focus on "you." For instance, don't say, *"You are annoying me"*; instead, use the I-statement *"I need space right now."* Listeners respond better to I-statements because they aren't put on the defensive.

- **Use "if-then" statements.** If someone crosses your boundaries, address them head-on by saying, *"I am frustrated right now because . . ."* or *"I feel disrespected when . . ."* Follow these up with an "if" and a "then." It sounds like this: *"If this continues to happen, then I'll need to leave this conversation."* Or *"If you keep disrespecting me like this, then we can't hang out."* These statements are clear, fair, and a mature way to reset your boundaries—a helpful skill for life, my friend.

DEAL WITH GROUP CONFLICTS

What do you do when your group of friends or classmates disagrees?

Some situations can simply be ignored. If someone is being annoying on purpose, they're most likely just looking for attention. Walk away if you can.

Sometimes, you'll need to speak up. Speaking up for yourself or others is not always easy. It's especially hard to go against a group if you look up to them or value their friendship. And who wants to be the odd man out? But sometimes speaking up is the right thing to do.

For small, manageable disagreements with a group (like in a group project in school), you'll need to use your words to stand up for yourself.

1. Use I-statements to express your feelings. Try *"I'm worried we won't finish. Can we please focus on the assignment?"*

2. If things turn ugly, redirect the focus. Use *"Whoa, not cool. I don't like when you talk like that—it feels disrespectful. Let's keep working."*

3. Keep trying. Speaking up comes more easily with practice. Come to an agreement if you can. If not, ask an adult for help.

Then there's peer pressure—other kids trying to influence you to do something you may or may not want to do. Peer pressure can be positive; a group might inspire you to put your art on display. Negative peer pressure happens when friends or a social group try to steer you in the wrong direction.

If you're facing negative peer pressure, stick to the basics.

- Say no, walk away, or change the subject.

- Come up with an excuse. Try *"I can't. I don't want to get in trouble at home"* or *"Sorry, I know someone who got hurt doing that,"* or if it involves bullying, *"I wouldn't want someone to do that to me."*

- Trust your instincts and reach out to a trusted adult if needed.

USE SOCIAL MEDIA WISELY

The internet is an exciting and useful world. Think about all you use it for: keeping connected with friends and family, learning everything from dances to foreign languages, playing music and games, tracking your physical activity, creating art—the choices are endless!

The internet can also be scary. For starters, online relationships might not be totally truthful. People can lie about their name, age, and other details. They might try to get information from you or ask for pictures and other personal information. This is not okay, and it's often illegal. Let a trusted adult know right away if anything feels strange or uncomfortable.

What skills do you need to stay safe?

- **Keep your privacy antenna up.** Keep your settings private so only your direct friends can see your profile. Keep your last name, address, school name and location, phone number, birthday, and all other personal information off the internet. No stranger needs to know those things. Don't even send these details to a friend—other people might be able to see them.

- **Think long-term.** The internet is forever. What you post online leaves a virtual footprint. Even if texts, photos, or browsing history are deleted, all searches and postings are still traceable. And photos can be reposted and shared with people you don't know. When you apply for a job, your employer may check social media to learn about you; you don't want any negative posts from your past to keep you from getting the job!

- **Practice stranger danger.** Don't respond to texts or emails from someone you don't know. Don't click links or open attachments from an unknown source. Never, ever agree to meet someone in person who you just met online.

- **Don't follow the crowd.** Make your mental health a priority by limiting screen time to two hours a day. Just because others are on a certain site (or online at midnight) doesn't mean you have to be!

ENJOY TIME ALONE

Do you want more freedom or alone time? That's normal! Learning how to make room for alone time and what to do during alone time is a skill that will serve you well. When telling others you want to be alone, choose your words carefully so you don't accidentally hurt their feelings.

Here's how to set alone time and make the best of it:

1. Explain what you're doing. A simple explanation will help: *"I need time alone to rest and recharge."* Then set aside time—from a few minutes to an hour—to recharge.

2. Use your alone time to fill up empty energy reservoirs. What makes you happy? What strengthens you emotionally and mentally? Are you re-energized after daydreaming? Or being out in nature? Does art or music recharge your batteries? Does journaling free up mental and emotional space? Find your energizing superpower and build it up in your alone time.

ROLLER-COASTER FRIENDS

You know who they are—those friends who make you happy one day and furious the next. They're what you could call "roller-coaster friends." They add fun to life, but also stress and annoyance. You'll find that as you grow, friends will come and go. It makes life easier when you surround yourself with friends who you can count on to be steady and reliable. If you find yourself navigating daily ups and downs with a roller-coaster friend, take a step back. Hopefully the roller-coaster friend will grow their social skills and become a steady friend—until then, it's okay to skip that ride!

PART THREE
OUT IN THE WORLD

Now that you've learned life skills you can use at home and school, let's round things out with a focus on skills for successfully living in your community.

Part three covers skills you can use to navigate the world at large. These final chapters include skills that will help you become independent and confident, such as managing money (chapter 8), communicating effectively (chapter 9), and dealing with event preparation, travel, and plans with others (chapter 10).

CHAPTER 8

MONEY MAKES THE WORLD GO ROUND

- ☐ SPEND WISELY

- ☐ SAVE WISELY

- ☐ BUDGET

- ☐ UNDERSTAND AND MANAGE A BANK ACCOUNT

- ☐ LEAVE A TIP

- ☐ DONATE

SPEND WISELY

It's okay to spend money on fun things, as long as you don't get carried away and you buy what you need first. Here's how to spend wisely:

- **Look ahead at the week.** Think essentials: Do you need anything this week? Deodorant or shampoo? Money for a class trip? Set that amount aside.

- **Consider what's in store for the month.** What big events are coming up? If you plan ahead, your future self will thank you.

- **Stick with your long-term vision.** Try not to buy something just because it seems cool in the moment. Trends often disappear quickly, only to be replaced by another trend.

- **Be mindful of peer pressure.** If you have "fun funds" available, are you spending them on stuff you truly enjoy? Buying things to impress others can drain you of both money and emotions.

- **Be a smart shopper.** Keep your cash, debit card, and credit cards safe and out of sight. Look for sales and compare prices. Confirm the price you're paying, whether using cash or a debit or credit card. If you're paying in cash, open all dollar bills before handing them to the cashier. Make sure you get the right change. If you're using a debit card, protect your PIN (personal identification number), if you have one. Make sure no one is watching when you enter it on the keypad.

SAVE WISELY

As a kid, you've probably had a piggy bank or some other form of saving cash. Perhaps family members have given you gifts of money for birthdays or holidays, or maybe you get an allowance. Being smart with money is a super important life skill that allows you to make good choices about how to spend your hard-earned cash. It will help you through your entire life! Let's talk about some skills that will make you a smart money manager.

- **Decide what's necessary and what's fun.** This is the first essential of having a budget. Knowing the difference between "wants" and "needs" can help you save and spend wisely. Fun is okay! But ask yourself if you really *need* that phone upgrade, trendy accessory, or tech gadget. Are those items merely temporary *wants*? As you get older and more responsible for your own needs, you'll have to prioritize food, clothing, and education ahead of hobbies and social image.

- **Keep a long-term vision.** Patience is key to saving money. Your future self will be happy you didn't fritter away your money on little items now. Yeah, you can use your money to buy candy every time you go to the store, but if you focus on the long term, you can purchase a larger item you've had your eye on, get nice gifts for friends and family, or pay for activities or expenses that pop up.

- **Consider finding a balance.** If you get money and want to spend it right away, consider saving some and spending some. This way, you'll get to enjoy something now but still save up for something bigger later. The best way to save is to open a bank account in your name. You'll be able to see it grow and collect interest on the money. Plus, when your money is in the bank, you won't be able to access it as easily as you would if it were sitting in your wallet. We'll talk more about this in the coming pages.

BUDGET

A budget is a plan for managing money. It looks at the money you earn, save, and spend. Budgeting wisely is a lifelong skill.

Some adults follow a 40-30-20-10 rule when it comes to money: 40 percent of their money goes toward savings; 30 percent goes toward necessary items like food, rent, and bills; 20 percent goes toward entertainment; and 10 percent goes to charity.

You might prefer something even simpler, like a 30-60-10 split. In this case, 30 percent of your money is for savings, 60 percent for spending, and 10 percent for sharing. So, for instance, if a family member gives you 10 dollars, you would save 3 dollars, spend 6 dollars, and donate 1 dollar to a fundraiser or a cause you believe in.

Here are essential tools for setting a budget. Even if you don't have a steady income right now, these tools will be helpful in the future.

1. Write down the total money coming in (earnings) and total money going out (expenses) for one full month. Don't skip anything!

2. Create spending categories and track how much money you put into each category. (Examples might be snacks, clothes, video games, hangouts with friends.)

3. Consider your needs and wants to set short-term and long-term goals. (For example: *I will save all chore money from weeks one and three each month until summer so I can buy* _____.)

MONTHLY BUDGET

JAN.

SOURCE	AMOUNT
LAWN MOWING FOR NEIGHBORS	$212
ALLOWANCE	$50
	$262

CATEGORY	AMOUNT
SNACKS	$53.50
GAMES	$98.75
BOOKS	$2.25
TOTAL	**$154.50**

GOAL	AMOUNT
SNEAKER FUND $200.00	$93.75+$97.50= $191.25

4. Cut spending or make small changes to make your goals possible. (For example: *Instead of popcorn, candy, and soda at the movies, I will choose just one item. I will also hold off on buying any new video games until I save $_____.*)

5. Check back each month to see if you need to adjust anything. (For example: *In July I spent $_____ and saved $_____. In August I'd like to spend $_____ and save $_____, so I need to eliminate all purchases of _____.*)

UNDERSTAND AND MANAGE A BANK ACCOUNT

Want to open a bank account? You and your caregiver may decide to set up a custodial banking account. This type of account lets you save and build healthy financial habits with help from a trusted adult. Visit a local bank and ask about this type of account.

Here are some helpful banking terms you may learn about:

- **Checking account:** This account lets you write checks and withdraw cash that was put into the account.

- **Savings account:** This account stores your money that you aren't ready to use yet, often with the goal of saving more.

- **Debit card:** When you use a debit card, the bank immediately pulls that amount out of your account. If you get a debit card, decide whether you will carry it with you or store it at home until you need it.

- **Credit card:** When you use a credit card, you owe that money to the credit card company at a later date. It is money you will be in debt for—you have to pay it back, plus interest (if your payment is late), which is additional money you'll owe for using credit.

- **Password:** Create a strong password for online banking and a PIN—a personal identification number—for your debit card and/or bank account.

- **ATM (automated teller machine):** Here you can deposit money, withdraw money, and check your accounts. Tap your card or insert it into the machine, enter your PIN, follow the directions on the screen, and remember to get your card back at the end! Be aware that using ATMs at other banks might cost you extra fees.

LEAVE A TIP

In the United States, tips are usually given to service providers like restaurant servers, hairstylists, taxi and rideshare drivers, and people who deliver food, to name a few.

Knowing how much to tip depends on a couple of factors:

- How was the service? Customers tip around 15 percent for good service, 20 percent for very good service, and more for excellent service.

- What can you afford? Consider the tip in your budget *before* you make this kind of purchase. If you can't afford to give a 15 to 20 percent tip, can you choose a less expensive option?

To figure out a 20 percent tip, move the decimal of the purchase over one spot to the left, then multiply by two. For example, if a meal costs you $12.50, move the decimal over so you have 1.25. Then double 1.25 to get you to $2.50, which is 20 percent of $12.50.

DONATE

It might seem like a bad idea to give away money, especially if you worked hard to earn it. But there are benefits to sharing your money, as long as you don't give away more than you can afford. Donating to a cause helps others; it also has a positive impact on your self-worth. Plus, if we all share a mindset of kindness and charity, this can benefit society as a whole.

You can donate money through the mail, online, or in person. However you decide to donate, check in with your caregiver first to make sure that the organization you're donating to is legitimate. Sites like charitynavigator.org give ratings of different charities based on how much of every dollar goes directly to the intended recipients.

What causes do you care about? Here are some ideas:

- Animal rights

- The environment

- Social justice

- Medical research

- Education

- Mental health

- World hunger

- Disaster relief

HELLO, YOUNG ENTREPRENEUR!

You probably have skills that you can use to make money. If you receive cash for chores, that's a great start! You can also help out around your neighborhood. Ask nearby families or local businesses if they would pay you for lawn care (mowing, weeding, etc.), help with the elderly, pet-walking or pet-sitting, babysitting, or computer-generated work like video creation or graphic design. You can also sell gently used items online! Check with your caregiver before putting anything for sale on the internet so they can help you with pricing, shipping, safety, and other considerations.

CHAPTER 9

SAY WHAT YOU MEAN, MEAN WHAT YOU SAY

- COMMUNICATE ONLINE

- MAKE AND RECEIVE PHONE CALLS

- TEXT WITH CARE

- EMAIL WITH CARE

- WRITE A THANK-YOU NOTE

- USE GOOD MANNERS

COMMUNICATE ONLINE

Before we even get to talking about online communication, let's start off by stating the obvious: Don't share passwords for your computer, email, phone, online/cloud drives, and websites. Change passwords often, using numbers and symbols as well as uppercase and lowercase letters to stay as safe as possible from scammers. Avoid commonly known details about you—you know, the stuff that others might guess, like your birthday, your pet's name, your street address, and so on.

A big problem with being online is that the information you see isn't always accurate. Some information is misleading or wrong; other information is just plain mean or damaging. It's important not to add to that. Always remember, who you are online is not different from who you are in real life. How can you be smart online and stay true to yourself? Use the THINK acronym as an online skill.

Is what you are viewing or sharing online:

TRUE? To the best of your knowledge, is it factual or just an opinion?

HELPFUL? Does the message help you, others, or the situation?

INSPIRING? Is the message a positive one?

NECESSARY? Is it necessary to pass along, especially for safety reasons? Or would the message be better left unsent?

KIND? Is the communication polite?

See chapter 7 (page 100) for more important skills for staying safe and smart online.

MAKE AND RECEIVE PHONE CALLS

Communicating by phone is an important social skill. How else are you going to order a pizza or wish Grandma a happy birthday?

1. **Move to a quiet, uncrowded place.** A crowded spot has too much background noise, and a quiet public area is no good either, since you might disrupt the people around you.

2. **Introduce yourself.** When you place a call and the person answers, say hello and identify yourself. State your reason for calling. If you're receiving a call, answer the phone and say hello.

3. **Speak clearly.** This is especially important on a cell phone out in the world, since background noise may make you harder to hear and understand.

4. **Avoid sarcasm.** Since you can't see expressions or body language over the phone, speak with a genuine tone. You can still joke and use your normal sense of humor, but remember that it doesn't always work well without facial expressions.

5. **Leave kindly but firmly.** If you want or need to hang up but the person on the other end is still talking, it's okay to say, *"I'm sorry, I have to go."* You can add, *"Can we please talk later?"*

6. **Say goodbye.** Do this nice and clearly, to signal the call is ending. Plain and simple, it's polite—even with good friends. Consider adding a *"Thanks for the call!"* to show gratitude for their time.

7. **Leave a message.** If nobody answers, after the beep, state your name, the time of day you called, what you wanted to talk about, and your phone number so they can call you back.

TEXT WITH CARE

Texting safely and properly is a skill! Even though text messages are usually casual, it still matters how you represent yourself.

- **Be clear and honest.** You can't see faces through text messages. It's even harder to read context, mood, and emotions. Be straightforward to avoid misunderstandings.

- **Read and reread.** It's easy to text quickly, but be careful—you can't take back what you sent. Look over your message to correct typos and ensure it is clear and appropriate.

- **Watch the clock.** Don't send messages too early in the morning or too late at night.

- **Limit mass texts.** In a group chat? Limit mass texts and spamming others in the group with too many messages. Remember that anything you type might be shared with others outside the group.

- **Be thoughtful.** Use the THINK acronym (page 119) to protect yourself and your reputation. Also, many parents check their kids' phones, so consider the words you use.

- **Don't text angry.** If you're angry or frustrated, don't communicate via text. Save the conversation for an in-person discussion.

EMAIL WITH CARE

Like texting, email can be casual—but it depends on the message and who you are writing to.

- **Know your audience.** Emailing a friend is different than emailing a teacher. Write more formally with adults and avoid acronyms (LOL, BTW, TTYL, etc.).

- **Write a helpful subject line.** Let your recipient know what your email is about (example: *Homework question*).

- **Use proper openings and closings.** *"Dear _____,"* or *"Hello _____"* work perfectly well. At the end, try *"Thanks for reading! Sincerely, _____."* If you're emailing a business, start with *"Dear Sir/Madam."* Use correct titles, if you know them: Mr., Ms., Dr., etc.

- **Never write an email angry or frustrated.** Emotional reactions never go well online. Breathe, calm down, and tone down your words. Don't write anything you wouldn't say to their face. If you're fighting with a friend, plan to meet in person to resolve your dispute.

- **Read and reread.** Make sure the message is clear and accurate before sending.

WRITE A THANK-YOU NOTE

When someone invests the time and money to give you a gift or does you a favor, a handwritten letter is a great way to say thank you. A thank-you note does not need to be super formal. Just speak from the heart to show your gratitude.

1. Start with *"Dear (gift-giver's name),"*.

2. Thank the person for the gift or favor.

3. Say how much you liked it and why (*"I love it because I've always wanted this book!"*) or how it helped you, and any other feelings that feel natural to include.

4. Phrases like *"I appreciate how you _____"* or *"It meant a lot that you helped me _____"* make the reader feel good about what they did for you.

2-12

Dear Aunt Jackie,

Thanks so much for giving me the next book i favorite series for birthday. I've been to see what happen last book ended on cliffhanger! So I can' to find out what happ next. I appreciate that always pay attention t what I'm interested in...

Love, Max

MAX PILCHARD
3859 24TH ST
SAN FRANCISCO, CA 94114

JACKIE PILCHARD
274 OAK ST
SIOUX FALLS, SD 57106

5. You can end your letter with *"Love, (your name)"* if you're writing to a family member or good friend. *"Your friend, (your name)"* works too, or *"Thanks again, (your name)"* if you're not close to the recipient. *"Sincerely,"* works too.

6. To address an envelope, write the address you're sending it to in the very center of the front of the envelope in this way:

FIRST NAME   LAST NAME
STREET ADDRESS (INCLUDING ANY APARTMENT NUMBER)
CITY,   STATE   ZIP CODE

Find and use the two-letter state abbreviation. To send letters overseas, add the country and other details (like extra numbers and letters) in the last line. You'll also need additional postage, so ask for the right stamp(s) at the post office.

The stamp(s) go in the upper right-hand corner of the envelope. Write your address in the upper left corner in the same format as your "To" address. This is done in case your letter is undeliverable and needs to be returned to you.

USE GOOD MANNERS

Good manners are a basic skill, but they're a skill that reaps endless rewards (like getting what you want or getting invited again). If you're nice to someone, chances are good they'll be nice back. Do you want something? Asking for it nicely gives you a better chance of getting it.

- **Say "please" and "thank you."** These courtesies are totally appreciated; don't be afraid to say them twice.

- **Use eye contact.** Look the person in the eye. This shows you are genuine, confident, and interested.

- **Start with a handshake.** Be the first to offer your hand! Look them in the eye and smile. Grip their hand with your right hand—keep your fingers together and meet the base of their thumb with yours. Give a couple of quick, solid shakes and release your hand.

- **Don't interrupt.** Let the person finish their thought before you respond.

- **Wait to eat.** Wait until everyone has their food in front of them before you dig in. Some people begin their meal with a prayer; you can either pray along or bow your head and sit quietly.

- **Speak up.** Ask for items to be passed to you instead of reaching across a table to get them. Give compliments and thank the person who made the meal.

- **Honor personal space.** Respect others' personal space. Keep a reasonable distance from other people, even when waiting in lines.

- **Hold doors for others.** This is particularly true for the elderly, but really for anyone behind you who is about to enter or exit through a door.

- **Learn and practice consent** (page 96). See if the other person is agreeable to what you want. In the case of physical contact, never assume someone wants the same thing you do. If unsure, just ask! A question like *"Fist bump?"* is simple and to the point.

HELP . . . PLEASE!

An honest and straightforward approach is usually best when you ask for a favor. It might sound like this: *"Hey! So, I've never done this before. Can you lend me a hand?"* Or maybe even just, *"Can I ask a favor?"* Then explain what you're looking for. It's okay to say you're nervous. People generally understand and have been in your shoes. Just use your manners! Say please, show genuine thanks, and return the favor if they're ever in need.

CHAPTER 10
OUT AND ABOUT

- READ A MAP

- PACK A SUITCASE

- HOST A HANGOUT

- BE A GREAT GUEST

- WATCH A YOUNGER CHILD

- PICK AND WRAP A PRESENT

- TIE A NECKTIE

READ A MAP

If you have a smartphone, you may have a GPS map available on an app. If you don't have a phone or cell service, a paper map will work great, but you'll need to know how to read one. Both work if you're walking, biking, or being driven.

Whether using your phone or a printed map:

1. Find your current location and get a frame of reference by looking at the directions—north, south, east, and west. This will help you determine where you are in the world and where you're going.

2. Type the destination address into your app or have it available.

3. Zoom out to take a look at the entire journey before leaving. Even a brief glance at all the roads, exits, and turns can make for a smoother trip. Read the directions on your app or look them over on your printed map.

4. Is there a key or legend? This map feature shows you what the symbols mean. For instance, what does a dotted line mean? What about a tiny flag? The map's legend will tell you. Use the symbols that you need for your trip.

5. If you're the car's navigator, pay attention! Know the next move well ahead of time, if possible, and tell the driver. For example: *"In a few miles we're going to be turning right at exit 142."*

6. Lost? It happens! Can you review the last few steps to get back on track? Or do you need to stop and ask for directions? It's better to ask earlier rather than later in your trip. No need to panic; seek out a gas station or a friendly face along the way. Ask how to return to the last major road or intersection to get your bearings back.

PACK A SUITCASE

When packing a suitcase, think about how many days and nights you'll be gone. Make sure you have enough clean clothes for each day. If it's a long trip, pack at least one extra set of clothes just in case.

1. Lay all your items out before putting them in your bag.

2. Cut out all the unnecessary stuff.

3. Look at the weather report for your destination and pack for the weather. If you'll be near water, remember flip-flops and a bathing suit; if you're going somewhere cold, bring gloves, hat, and a coat.

4. Choose clothes and shoes that can be worn no matter what the situation.

5. Roll or fold clothing? Both! Roll softer materials that won't wrinkle and fold nicer items like dress clothes.

6. Use the empty space inside shoes for socks and underwear.

7. Protect delicate items like glasses by placing them in shoes or wrapping them in multiple shirts for padding.

8. Combine all toiletries—toothpaste, toothbrush, shampoo, sunscreen, and so on—in zip-top bags or a travel kit so they don't leak on your clothes.

9. Put all your clothing, toiletries, and other items inside your bag. Remove unnecessary items if your bag won't close.

10. If you're flying, read airline rules for both carry-ons and checked luggage. If you get to bring a carry-on, think about putting your phone, charger, something to read or do, and snacks in it.

HOST A HANGOUT

Whether you're hosting a party or just inviting buddies over to watch a movie, here are some basic guidelines for hosting a get-together.

1. If you're hosting a party, what's the occasion? Will you need decorations? Paper plates and napkins? Food and drinks? A theme? Make a list of the things you'll need to buy or make.

2. State a start and end time, even if it's okay if your friends arrive a bit earlier and stay a little later. If you want them at your home at 7 p.m., tell them so. If you need to have everyone out of your home by 10 p.m., just let them know!

3. Are you providing a meal or snacks? If you want your friends to bring food or drinks, give them some options. If not, let them know what you'll be serving (like pizza and soda, or just cake).

4. Are food allergies a concern? Ask your guests ahead of time so you can make a menu that keeps everyone safe.

5. Clean up the hangout area before people come over. Yes, my man—you'll want to make your bed, put your clothes away, and pick up clutter to make the place presentable. No one wants to sit by your dirty socks.

6. Greet your friends at the door. Offer to take their coats as needed.

7. Make sure everyone is introduced to everyone else.

8. Keep checking in on your friends. Make sure they don't need anything—a soda refill, different snack options—and let them know where the bathroom is.

9. Say goodbye, thank your friends for coming over, and walk them to the door. Make sure they leave with any personal items they came with.

10. Clean up! Wash dishes and put away any leftover food. Sweep the floor and clean up any spills. Try to return the area to the way it looked before; it's the right thing to do, and your caregivers might be more agreeable to future parties!

BE A GREAT GUEST

It's not hard to be a gracious visitor. Just think about what you like when friends hang out at your place, and act that way at their place. Keep these guidelines in mind:

- RSVP as soon as you can. This helps the host plan.

- Stick to your commitment. Last-minute cancellations are disappointing (and rude).

- Offer to bring something to eat or drink. Once you're there, offer to help out in some way.

- Arrive on time, but not too early.

- Talk with as many people as you're comfortable with. Say hi and interact with the host for a while.

- Feel free to eat and drink, but don't overindulge.

- Respect the host's home. Should you take your shoes off? Would a coaster be best on their table? Resist the urge to put your feet on the furniture or lie on the couch! Offer to help clean up.

- Thank the host and say goodbye before you leave.

WATCH A YOUNGER CHILD

At some point, you'll probably end up watching a child. Maybe a neighbor asks you to babysit, or perhaps you're at a family event with a younger cousin who wants your attention. Caring for another person is a big deal! It's an important and rewarding life skill. Let's explore the basics.

- **Put safety first.** Make sure the child is safe by staying with them at all times, keeping them occupied with games and toys designed for kids their age, and helping them with any needs they have, such as feeding them or grabbing an out-of-reach toy for them.

- **Engage them.** Don't be afraid to get silly and "on their level." Use your imagination to build, create, and play together. Pillow and cushion forts can make for hours of fun.

- **Have a parent's number.** If the child becomes unruly or upset, try doing a quiet activity together like reading a book. If they don't settle down, it's okay to contact the parents to let them know or ask for advice.

PICK AND WRAP
A PRESENT

This can be a toughie, my man. But picking out the right present and wrapping it shows you care. Let's brainstorm!

- Do you share common interests? How about an inside joke?

- Would they like something you created? Do you make art or music? Would they want a photo or keepsake from time spent together?

- What do they need? Is there something they'd like but wouldn't buy for themselves?

- Would they like to share an experience with you? Would they like to go for a hike together? Visit a museum with you? Make your own "gift certificate" announcing your plan.

The easiest way to wrap a present is to place it in a gift bag with decorative tissue. This method is great for oddly shaped gifts—have you ever tried to wrap a basketball?

If you want to use wrapping paper:

1. Bring the present, wrapping paper, scissors, and tape to the table.

2. Unroll some wrapping paper facedown. Place the box in the center, upside down. Bring the paper up and over, making sure it overlaps a bit where it meets. Also make sure there are a couple of extra inches on each end. Cut the paper around the present.

3. Bring the long sides of the paper up and over so they overlap, and use one or two pieces of tape to tape them down.

4. Starting on one short end, push and fold down the top flap onto the side of the box, creating two little wings (that look like triangles) at the side. Flatten the wing triangles inward, then pull the bottom flap up and tape it down. Repeat on the other side. This takes practice— and it doesn't have to look perfect!

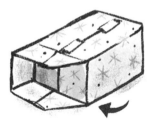

5. Turn the box over so the taped side faces down. Tape a bow on top. Add the recipient's name to a gift tag or card and tape it to the top.

TIE A NECKTIE

Getting dressed up for a big event? There are a few ways to tie a tie. Here's a basic one:

1. Place the tie around your neck by turning up your collar, putting the center of the tie under it (seam side in), then folding the collar back down over the tie. The ends will be hanging down in the front.

2. Pull the wide end down a tad lower than the narrow end.

3. Cross the wide end over the narrow end, then pull the wide end behind.

4. Cross the wide end over again, up high so it crosses to form the front of the knot. Pull up behind and through at your neck. The wide end should hang in front of the narrow end.

5. Pick the wide end up to see the loop at the front of the knot. Slide the tie through the loop. Use one hand to pull the wide end down while the other hand keeps the knot tight up by your neck. Wiggle and center the tie at your collar as needed.

6. Check the length: The tip of the wide part of the tie should hit the top of your belt buckle. If not, redo, adjusting the length at the start (step 2) and the height of your hold on the knot as it's forming (steps 4 and 5).

WHY'D THE CHICKEN CROSS THE ROAD?

The world is a busy place. Whether you live in the country or the city, you'll eventually need to cross a busy intersection. When you're walking or biking in the street, imagine that car drivers can't see you. This way, you'll be extra careful. If there is a traffic light, wait to cross the road until the light turns red and traffic stops. If there's no traffic light, wait for a very wide clearing to cross. Never text or stop on the street (even if you drop something—your life is more important than any object). Safe travels!

ACKNOWLEDGMENTS

I am immensely grateful for the chance to help young people and their families shine the spotlight on the greatest show on earth: life.

I appreciate all the opportunities I am afforded to connect with other like-minded people at various points in their life story. Health, education, writing, and media creation continue to inspire me and offer the chance to learn more than I ever imagined. I am in debt to my fellow educators and leading organizations helping to push for comprehensive health programs and accessible, appropriate resources for kids and teens.

Special thanks go out to my wife, Sarah, for understanding all of the late nights and early mornings it takes to pursue the written word. Thanks to my amazing kids for weekly movie nights and constant inside jokes. Thanks to all the parents and caregivers supporting this book and similar publications. And, as always, the biggest thanks go out to you, the reader, for putting your trust in these chapters. I hope any days of struggle bring years of success.

ABOUT THE AUTHOR

SCOTT TODNEM has been teaching health education at the middle school level since 2001 and was named the 2019 National Health Teacher of the Year. He uses his platforms to promote cultural diversity, gender inclusivity, mental health awareness, and suicide prevention. He is also the author of *Growing Up Great! The Ultimate Puberty Book for Boys* and *Sex Education: A Parent's Guide.*

Scott hosts a YouTube channel and a podcast with his students, both of which can be found at lifeisthefuture.com. He currently resides in Illinois with his family, where he enjoys reading, record collecting, and watching great movies.

ABOUT THE ILLUSTRATOR

MARTHA SUE COURSEY is a San Francisco–based illustrator, type designer, and artist. She grew up as the only child of metalwork artists in a house they built on the outskirts of Tucson, Arizona, where books and desert creatures were some of her best friends. She holds a BFA in painting from California College of the Arts and a postgraduate certificate from Type West. When she's not drawing, she's taking care of too many plants or walking the dog. For more information, visit marthasuecoursey.com.